THE SCIENCE OF
BASKETBALL

By
William Anthony

KidHaven
PUBLISHING

PLAY
SMART

Published in 2021 by
KidHaven Publishing, an Imprint of Greenhaven Publishing, LLC
353 3rd Avenue
Suite 255
New York, NY 10010

© 2021 Booklife Publishing
This edition is published by arrangement with Booklife Publishing

Cataloging-in-Publication Data

Names: Anthony, William.
Title: The science of basketball / William Anthony.
Description: New York : KidHaven Publishing, 2021. | Series: Play
smart | Includes glossary and index.
Identifiers: ISBN 9781534535640 (pbk.) | ISBN 9781534535664
(library bound) | ISBN 9781534535657 (6 pack) | ISBN
9781534535671 (ebook)
Subjects: LCSH: Basketball--Juvenile literature. | Sports sciences--
Juvenile literature.
Classification: LCC GV885.1 A584 2021 | DDC 796.323--dc23

Printed in the United States of America

CPSIA compliance information: Batch #BS20K: For further information contact
Greenhaven Publishing LLC, New York, New York, at 1-844-317-7404.

Please visit our website, www.greenhavenpublishing.com.
For a free color catalog of all our high-quality books,
call toll free 1-844-317-7404 or fax 1-844-317-7405.

Find us on

Photo credits:
Cover – glenda, Monkey Business Images, Torsak Thammachote, naito29, FocusStocker, artproem, 2 – Fernando Cruz, 4 –
LDWYTN, 5 – Monkey Business Images, 6 – Alex Kravtsov, 7 – GotziLA STOCK, 8 – Ebitkar, 9 – oneinchpunch, 10 – Phovoir, 11 –
Ivica Drusany, 12 – Petur Asgeirsson, 13 – Yuriy Golub, 14 – Boris Ryaposov, 15 – icsnaps, 17 – Trong Nguyen, 18 – OSTILL is Franck
Camhi, 19 – oneinchpunch, 20 – Ljupco Smokovski, 21 – Gino Santa Maria, Yuriy Golub, Nicholas Piccillo.

Images are courtesy of Shutterstock.com. With thanks to Getty Images, Thinkstock Photo, and iStockphoto.

All facts, statistics, web addresses, and URLs in this book were verified as valid and accurate at time of writing.
No responsibility for any changes to external websites or references can be accepted by either the author or publisher.

CONTENTS

Words that look like **this** can be found in the glossary on page 24.

GET ON THE COURT!

Do you want to learn all about the angles, **forces**, and patterns that go into a game of basketball? The game is about to start, so lace up your high-tops and grab the ball!

Basketball is a game in which two teams of five players compete against each other to score points. Points are scored by shooting the ball through the hoop that the other team is defending.

HOOP

OFFENSIVE PLAYER

DEFENDER

Shots made near the basket are worth two points. Shots made from behind the three-point line are worth three.

DIRECT DRIBBLING

KEEP YOUR BACK STRAIGHT

Bending your knees will give you a low **center of gravity**, making it easier to turn quickly and keep control of the ball.

BEND YOUR KNEES

When your team goes on offense, you'll be dribbling from one end of the court to the other. You do this by bouncing the ball on the ground beside you as you travel forward.

In basketball, you must bounce the ball when you are moving around the court. When you bounce the ball, you push it toward the ground. When the ball hits the floor, it **compresses** and rebounds back upward into your hand.

PUSH AND GRAVITY

BALL PUSHED INTO THE AIR

As the ball bounces, some of the energy pushes it back upward. However, some energy is lost because of **friction** and **air resistance**.

BRILLIANT BOUNCE PASS

If you have an **opponent** guarding you, a bounce pass to get the ball to another player might be a good choice. This is when you bounce the ball off the ground to your teammate.

SMALLER ANGLE FOR A CLOSER TEAMMATE

If your teammate is close by, bounce the ball at a smaller angle. If your teammate is farther away, the angle will need to be bigger.

To pass to a teammate farther away, you will need to put more force into your pass to make sure the ball has enough energy to reach them.

BIGGER ANGLE FOR A TEAMMATE FARTHER AWAY

CHEST PASS CHAMPION

If there are no opponents between you and your teammate, you could try a chest pass. Chest passes are normally more **accurate** than bounce passes.

To make a chest pass, bend your elbows and hold the ball near your chest, then push the ball away from you.

BALL NEXT TO CHEST

BENT ELBOWS

EYES

Extend your arms as much as you can to increase the speed of your chest pass.

The more you bend your elbows, the more **potential energy** you store. When you push the ball to make the pass, the potential energy is transferred from your arms into the ball, making it move toward your teammate.

FANCY FOOTWORK

If the player has both hands on the ball, they have to stop running.

PIVOT FOOT

It's hard to make a pass when you're surrounded by defenders. To get out of trouble, you can keep one foot in place and use the other to spin around. This is called **pivoting**.

USE THE PIVOTING MOTION TO KEEP THE BALL AS FAR AWAY FROM THE DEFENDER AS POSSIBLE.

Defenders will make big shapes with their bodies to block an offensive player.

PIVOT FOOT

You can move your free foot around to the left or to the right to get around a defender.

SHARP SHOOTING

When you get close enough to the other team's hoop, it's time to take a shot. There are lots of shapes and angles that go into the perfect shot.

BEND YOUR SHOOTING ARM INTO TWO RIGHT ANGLES, ONE AT YOUR ELBOW AND ONE AT YOUR WRIST, AS IF YOU WERE TRYING TO MAKE THREE SIDES OF A SQUARE.

LOOK UPWARD AND FORWARD TOWARD THE HOOP.

YOUR ARM SHOULD LOOK LIKE A SWAN'S NECK!

PUSHING UP WITH YOUR KNEES HELPS TO FORCE THE BALL HIGH INTO THE AIR.

Jumping pushes you high into the air.

After you've taken aim, push up from your knees and extend your arm into a long, straight line. Just as you release the ball, flick your hand toward the hoop to make the ball move forward.

OFF THE BACKBOARD

LOW PRESSURE

Backspin gives the ball extra **lift**, which creates a better arc shape for your shot.

BALL PUSHED FORWARD

DIRECTION OF SPIN

HIGH PRESSURE

When you flick your wrist toward the hoop during your shot, you will put backspin on the ball. This creates an area of low **air pressure** above the ball and high air pressure below it.

When the basketball hits the backboard, the backspin helps the ball to drop down through the hoop, rather than bouncing away.

BALL FALLS DOWNWARD

FRICTION

BACKSPIN MAKES THE BALL SPIN TOWARD THE GROUND.

When the ball touches the backboard, friction is created. The backspin and the energy lost through friction make the ball fall downward.

DEADLY DEFENSE

Keeping your knees bent gives you potential energy, meaning you are always ready to jump, move, or block a shot.

DEFENDER

OFFENSIVE PLAYER

When your team is defending, your task is to stop the offensive team from working their way toward the hoop and scoring points. Just like when you're on offense, keeping a low center of gravity is important

When you're trying to stop your opponent from passing or shooting, taking up a lot of space will make it harder for them. Spread your arms out wide, and separate your feet to cover a big area.

SPREAD OUT YOUR ARMS

STAND WITH FEET APART

Taking up space with your body gives the offensive player less space to pass or move into.

WHAT'S NEXT?

When you're defending, guessing your opponent's next move will help you make a block. Thinking like an offensive player will help you play better defense.

Take a look at this offensive player. If you were defending against her, what position would you get into?

Would it be position 1, 2, or 3? Remember to think about whether she is getting ready to make a chest pass, a bounce pass, or a shot.

1

2

3

MAKE THE BLOCK

That's right, it's position 2. Get ready to jump and stretch your arms, because she's about to shoot! Let's take a look at the science behind the shot.

DIRECTION

Her eyes are looking upward and forward. This means she is probably looking toward the hoop in front of her. Position 1 is too low to stop this shot. It would be more suited to blocking a bounce pass.

ANGLES

Her arms are starting to make right angles. This means she is getting ready to take a shot. Position 2 is perfect for jumping high in the air and blocking the ball!

ENERGY

Her knees are bent, so she is storing potential energy, which will help her jump. This means you're going to have to jump too if you want to block her shot! Position 3 is good, but you won't be high enough in the air to stop her from scoring!

IT'S VERY IMPORTANT TO LOOK AT YOUR OPPONENT WHEN PLAYING, INSTEAD OF JUST LOOKING AT THE BALL. THIS IS CALLED "PLAYING THE PLAYER, NOT THE BALL."

GLOSSARY

accurate	precise and careful
air pressure	the force air puts on any surface in contact with it
air resistance	the frictional force air creates against a moving object, slowing it down
center of gravity	the point at which the weight of something is balanced
compresses	squeezes something using pressure
forces	pushes or pulls on an object
friction	when one object rubs against another
lift	an upward force
opponent	a member of another team playing against you
pivoting	turning around a fixed point
potential energy	the amount of energy stored inside an object that is ready to be used

INDEX